Uriah Furman Rogers

A Pictured Compilation of Hymns

Loved and Sung by Christians the World Over

Uriah Furman Rogers

A Pictured Compilation of Hymns
Loved and Sung by Christians the World Over

ISBN/EAN: 9783744779005

Printed in Europe, USA, Canada, Australia, Japan

Cover: Foto ©Thomas Meinert / pixelio.de

More available books at **www.hansebooks.com**

A Pictured Compilation of Hymns
Loved and Sung By Christians
the world over

✝

Uriah Furman Rogers
Compiler and Publisher

✝

155 West 97th Street
New York City

PRESS OF J. K. RICHARDSON
29 Pearl St., New York.

"'Tis finished!" so the Saviour cried,
And meekly bowed his head and died:
"'Tis finished!"—yes, the race is run,
The battle fought, the victory won.

'Tis finished!—all that heaven foretold
By prophets in the days of old;
And truths are opened to our view
That kings and prophets never knew.

'Tis finished!—Son of God, Thy power
Hath triumphed in this awful hour;
And yet our eyes with sorrow see
That life to us was death to Thee.

'Tis finished!—let the joyful sound
Be heard through all the nations round;
'Tis finished!—let the triumph rise,
And swell the chorus of the skies.

Behold the Lamb of God!
O, Thou for sinners slain,
Let it not be in vain
       That Thou hast died:
Thee for my Saviour let me take,
My only refuge let me make
       Thy pierced side.

Behold the Lamb of God!
Into the sacred flood
Of Thy most precious blood
       My soul I cast :
Wash me and make me clean within,
And keep me pure from every sin,
       Till life be past.

Behold the Lamb of God!
All hail, incarnate Word,
Thou everlasting Lord,
       Saviour most blest;
Fill us with love that never faints,
Grant us with all Thy blessed saints,
       Eternal rest.

Behold the Lamb of God!
Worthy is He alone,
That sitteth on the throne
       Of God above ;
One with the Ancient of all days,
One with the Comforter in praise,
       All light and love.

Upon the Gospel's sacred page
  The gathered beams of ages shine;
And, as it hastens, every age
  But makes its brightness more divine.

On mightier wing, in loftier flight,
  From year to year does knowledge soar;
And, as it soars, the Gospel light
  Becomes effulgent more and more.

More glorious still, as centuries roll,
  New regions blest, new powers unfurled,
Expanding with the expanding soul,
  Its radiance shall o'erflow the world,--

Flow to restore, but not destroy;
  As when the cloudless lamp of day
Pours out its floods of light and joy,
  And sweeps the lingering mist away.

" It is the theology of the heart that invites men
Our very childhood is embalmed in sacred tunes
and hymns. Our early lives, and the lives of our
parents, hang in the atmosphere of sacred song."

Mary, the pure and lowly maid, the favored of the Lord.

Now, the blessèd Dayspring
    Cometh from on high;
Now, the world's Redeemer,
    To her aid, draws nigh ;
Bearer of the tidings,
    From the throne of light,
To a lowly maiden,
    Speeds an angel bright.

In the chosen daughter
    Of King David's line,
God fulfills the promise
    Of King Ahaz's sign:
Gabriel hath spoken;
    Mary hath believed;
And, behold a virgin
    Hath a Son conceived.

Though He take our nature
    Linked to low estate,
Though He stoop to suffer,
    Yet shall He be great;
Though His crown and sceptre
    Be of thorn and reed,
His shall be the kingdom
    Sworn to David's Seed.

Light to light the Gentiles
    Bending at His throne;
Glory of His people,
    When His sway they own ;
He shall reign forever,
    King of kings confessed,
And all tribes and kindreds
    Shall, in Him, be blest.

Hark! what mean those holy voices
　　Sweetly sounding through the skies?
Lo! the angelic host rejoices,
　　Heavenly alleluias rise.

Listen to the wondrous story,
　　Which they chant in hymns of joy—
"Glory in the highest, glory!
　　Glory be to God most high!

"Peace on earth, good-will from heaven,
　　Reaching far as man is found;
Souls redeemed and sins forgiven,
　　Loud our golden harps shall sound.

"Christ is born; the great Anointed!
　　Heaven and earth His praises sing!
Oh, receive Whom God appointed
　　For your Prophet, Priest, and King!

"Hasten, mortals, to adore Him;
　　Learn His name to magnify,
Till in heaven ye sing before Him,
　　Glory be to God most high!"

Rejoice ye sons of men!
Your brightest praises yield!
The everlasting Son
See in the flesh revealed!
The world's Redeemer comes to-day
His own redemption's price to pay!

Lo! Simeon's saintly arms
The holy burden bear;
He sees with raptured eye
His true salvation there.
The weary waiting now is past:
The long-expected comes at last.

The agèd saint's embrace
The blessèd mother saw,
And on his words so strange
She mused with silent awe.
What conflict for her child is stored?
And what for her this piercing sword?

O Saviour, in Thy courts
We all our sins confess:
But Thou didst once for us
Fulfill all righteousness.
Impure, unclean, oh, may we be
Presented pure and clean in Thee!

And when, O God made Man,
Upon our waiting eye,
In glorious might revealed,
Salvation draweth nigh;
In that great day Thy servants bless,
And be "the Lord our Righteousness!"

As with gladness men of old
Did the guiding star behold;
As with joy they hailed its light,
Leading onward beaming bright;
So most gracious Lord, may we
Evermore be led to Thee.

As with joyful steps they sped
To that lowly manger-bed;
There to bend the knee before
Him whom heaven and earth adore;
So may we with willing feet
Ever seek the mercy-seat.

As they offered gifts most rare
At that manger rude and bare;
So may we with holy joy,
Pure and free from sin's alloy,
All our costliest treasures bring,
Christ! to Thee our heavenly King.

Holy Jesus! every day
Keep us in the narrow way;
And, when earthly things are past,
Bring our ransomed souls at last
Where they need no star to guide,
Where no clouds Thy glory hide.

In the heavenly country bright,
Need they no created light;
Thou its Light, its Joy, its Crown,
Thou its Sun which goes not down,
There forever may we sing
Alleluias to our King.

A pilgrim through this lonely world,
    The blessèd Saviour passed;
A mourner all his life was He,
    A dying Lamb at last.

That tender heart that felt for all,
    For all its life blood gave;
It found on earth no resting-place,
    Save only in the grave.

Such was our Lord; and shall we fear
    The cross, with all its scorn?
Or love a faithless evil world,
    That wreathed his brow with thorn?

No! facing all its frowns or smiles,
    Like him, obedient still,
We homeward press thro' storm or calm,
    To Zion's blessèd hill.

Then was fulfilled that which was spoken by Jeremy the prophet, saying, In Rama was there a voice heard, lamentation, and weeping, and great mourning, Rachel weeping for her children, and would not be comforted because they are not.

Once in royal David's city
    Stood a lowly cattle shed,
Where a mother laid her baby,
    In a manger for His bed;
Mary was that mother mild,
Jesus Christ her little child.

He came down to earth from heaven,
    Who is God and Lord of all,
And His shelter was a stable,
    And His cradle was a stall;
With the poor, and mean, and lowly,
Lived on earth our Saviour holy.

And, through all His wondrous childhood,
    He would honor and obey,
Love and watch the lowly maiden
    In whose gentle arms He lay :
Christian children all must be
Mild, obedient, good as He.

For He is our childhood's pattern;
    Day by day like us He grew :
He was little, weak and helpless,
    Tears and smiles like us He knew ;
And He feeleth for our sadness,
And He shareth in our gladness.

And our eyes at last shall see Him,
    Through His own redeeming love ;
For that child so dear and gentle
    Is our Lord in heaven above,
And He leads His children on
To the place where He is gone.

Not in that poor lowly stable,
    With the oxen standing by,
We shall see Him ; but in heaven,
    Set at God's right hand on high ;
When like stars His children crowned,
All in white shall wait around.

HE SHALL BE CALLED A NAZARENE.

Within the Father's house
  The Son hath found His home;
And to His temple suddenly
  The Lord of Life hath come.

The doctors of the law
  Gaze on the wondrous child,
And marvel at His gracious words
  Of wisdom undefiled.

Yet not to them is given
  The mighty truth to know,
To lift the earthly veil which hides
  Incarnate God below.

The secret of the Lord
  Escapes each human eye,
And faithful pondering hearts await
  The full Epiphany.

Lord, visit Thou our souls
  And teach us by Thy grace,
Each dim revealing of Thyself
  With loving awe to trace ;

Till from our darkened sight
  The cloud shall pass away,
And on the cleansèd soul shall burst
  The everlasting day;

Till we behold Thy face,
  And know, as we are known,
Thee, Father, Son and Holy Ghost,
  Co-equal Three in One.

O Son divine! we fain would trace
   Thy mother's steps so lowly,
Her joys and woes, her saintly grace,
   Her life so calm and holy.

But lo! as all too near we press,
   A veil the scene enfoldeth!
No tongue may sing its loveliness,
   No eye its peace beholdeth.

BUT MARY KEPT ALL THESE THINGS, AND PONDERED
THEM IN HER HEART.

On Jordan's bank the Baptist's cry
Announces that the Lord is nigh ;
Awake, and hearken, for he brings
Glad tidings of the King of kings.

Then cleansed be every Christian breast,
And furnished for so great a guest ;
Yea, let us each our hearts prepare
For Christ to come and enter there.

For Thou art our salvation, Lord,
Our refuge and our great reward ;
Without Thy grace we waste away,
Like flowers that wither and decay.

To heal the sick stretch out Thine hand,
And bid the fallen sinner stand ,
Once more upon thy people shine,
And fill the world with love divine.

All praise, eternal Son, to Thee,
Whose Advent set Thy people free ;
Whom with the Father we adore,
And Holy Ghost for evermore.

"THE KINGDOM OF HEAVEN IS AT HAND."

Thou didst leave Thy throne and Thy kingly crown,
  When Thou camest to earth for me ;
But in Bethlehem's home was there found no room
  For Thy holy Nativity.
    Oh, come to my heart, Lord Jesus!
    There is room in my heart for Thee.

Heaven's arches rang when the angels sang,
  Proclaiming Thy royal degree ;
But in lowly birth didst Thou come to earth,
  And in great humility.
    Oh, come to my heart, Lord Jesus!
    There is room in my heart for Thee.

The foxes found rest and the birds had their nest
  In the shade of the forest tree ;
But Thy couch was the sod, O Thou Son of God,
  In the desert of Galilee.
    Oh, come to my heart, Lord Jesus!
    There is room in my heart for Thee.

Thou camest, O Lord, with the living word,
  That should set Thy people free ;
But with mocking scorn, and with crown of thorn,
  They bore Thee to Calvary.
    Oh, come to my heart, Lord Jesus?
    Thy cross is my only plea.

When the heavens shall ring, and the angels sing
  At Thy coming to victory,
Let Thy voice call me home, saying, " Yet there is room,
  There is room at My side for thee."
    And my heart shall rejoice, Lord Jesus,
    When Thou comest and callest for me.

A tower of strength our God doth stand,
   A shield and sure defender;
True help from all our woes, His hand
   Through life doth freely render.
Our foe hath fixed his purpose fell,
With might and craft he's armed full well,
   On earth is not his fellow.

With force of arms we nothing can
   Full soon were we o'erridden ;
But for us fights the goodly Man
   Whom God Himself hath bidden.
Ask ye His Name? 'Tis Christ our Lord,
The God of Hosts alone adored,
   Our Champion, none dare brave Him.

Should hell's whole legion round us press,
   All banded to devour us,
Yet this should work us good success,
   Nor fear e'en then o'erpower us ;
Though this world's prince look fierce and bold,
It matters not, his doom is told,
   A single word can foil him.

Our foes must let the Word stand sure ;
   No thanks for this they're reaping ;
God's Spirit in His way secure,
   God's grace our souls is keeping ;
Those foes may spoil all earthly bliss ;
Let be! they win no gain from this,
   God's kingdom still is left us.

Then the devil leaveth Him, and behold angels came and ministered unto Him.

Songs of thankfulness and praise
Jesu, Lord, to Thee we raise,
Manifested by the star
To the sages from afar ;
Branch of royal David's stem
In thy birth at Bethlehem ;
Anthems be to Thee addressed,
God in Man made manifest.

Manifest at Jordan's stream,
Prophet, Priest, and King supreme ;
And at Cana, wedding-guest,
In Thy Godhead manifest;
Manifest in power divine,
Changing water into wine ;
Anthems be to Thee addressed,
God in Man made manifest.

" BEHOLD, THE LAMB OF GOD!"

Thou spakest: it was done:
   Obedient to thy word
The water reddening into wine
   Proclaimed the present Lord.

Blest were the eyes which saw
   That wondrous mystery ;
The great beginning of Thy works,
   That kindled faith in Thee.

Would you win a soul to God?
Tell him of a Saviour's blood,
Once for dying sinners spilt
To atone for all their guilt.

Tell him,—it was sovereign grace
Led thee first to seek his face;
Made thee choose the better part,
Wrought salvation in thy heart.

Tell him of that liberty
Wherewith Jesus makes thee free;
Sweetly speak of sins forgiven,
Earnest of the joys of heaven.

Jesus calls us ; o'er the tumult
  Of our life's wild, restless sea,
Day by day His sweet voice soundeth,
  Saying, "Christian, follow Me."

As of old, Saint Andrew heard it
  By the Gal ean lake,
Turned from home, and toil and kindred,
  Leaving all for His dear sake.

Jesus calls us from the worship
  Of the vain world's golden store ;
From each idol that would keep us,
  Saying, "Christian, love Me more."

In our joys and in our sorrows,
  Days of toil and hours of ease,
Still He calls, in cares and pleasures,
  "That we love Him more than these."

Jesus calls us: by Thy mercies,
  Saviour, make us hear Thy call,
Give our hearts to Thine obedience,
  Serve and love Thee best of all.

Come, ye sinners, poor and wretched,
  Weak and wounded, sick and sore,
Jesus ready stands to save you,
  Full of pity, love and power.
      He is able,
  He is willing, doubt no more.

Let not conscience make you linger,
  Nor of fitness fondly dream:
All the fitness He requireth
  Is to feel your need of Him ;
      This He gives you ;
  'Tis the Spirit's rising beam.

Agonizing in the garden,
  Lo! your Maker prostrate lies;
On the bloody tree behold Him,
  Hear Him cry before He dies:
      "It is finished ;"
  Sinners, will not this suffice?

Lo! th' incarnate God ascended,
  Pleads the merit of His blood ;
Venture on Him, venture wholly ;
  Let no other trust intrude:
      None but Jesus
  Can do helpless sinners good.

JESUS SAITH UNTO HIM, "RISE, TAKE UP THY
BED AND WALK."

Lord, I am come! Thy promise is my plea,
  Without Thy word I durst not venture nigh;
But Thou hast called the burdened soul to Thee,
  A weary, burdened soul, O Lord, am I!

Bowed down beneath a heavy load of sin,
  By Satan's fierce temptations sorely prest,
Beset without and full of fears within,
  Trembling and faint I come to Thee for rest.

Be Thou my refuge, Lord, my hiding-place;
  I know no force can tear me from Thy side;
Unmoved, I then may all accusers face,
  And answer every charge, with—"Jesus died."

"COME UNTO ME AND I WILL GIVE YOU REST."

How condescending and how kind
    Was God's eternal Son!
Our misery reached His heavenly mind,
    And pity brought Him down.

He sunk beneath our heavy woes,
    To raise us to His throne;
There's ne'er a gift His hand bestows,
    But cost His heart a groan.

This was compassion, like a God,
    That when the Saviour knew
The price of pardon was His blood,
    His pity ne'er withdrew.

Now, though He reigns exalted high,
    His love is still as great;
Well He remembers Calvary,
    Nor lets His saints forget.

"THE SABBATH WAS MADE FOR MAN, NOT MAN FOR THE SABBATH."

SILOAM.

"GO, WASH IN THE POOL OF SILOAM."

When, like a stranger on our sphere,
The lowly Jesus wandered here,
Where'er He went affliction fled,
And sickness reared her fainting head.

The eye that rolled in irksome night,
Beheld His face—for God is light ;
The opening ear, the loosened tongue,
His precepts heard, his praises sung.

With bounding steps the halt and lame,
To hail their great Deliverer came ;
O'er the cold grave he bowed His head,
He spake the word, and raised the dead.

Despairing madness, dark and wild,
In His inspiring presence smiled;
The storm of horror ceased to roll,
And reason lightened through the soul.

Through paths of loving-kindness led,
Where Jesus triumphed we would tread ;
To all, with willing hands dispense
The gifts of our benevolence.

Go, labor on! spend and be spent!
　　Thy joy to do the Father's will;
It is the way the Master went;
　　Should not the servant tread it still?

Go, labor on! 'tis not for naught;
　　Thine earthly loss is heavenly gain;
Men heed thee, love thee, praise thee not;
　　The Master praises: what are men?

Go, labor on! enough, while here,
　　If He shall praise thee, if He deign
The willing heart to mark and cheer:
　　No toil for Him shall be in vain.

Go, labor on, while it is day!
　　The world's dark night is hastening on:
Speed, speed thy work! cast sloth away!
　　It is not thus that souls are won.

Toil on! faint not! keep watch, and pray!
　　Be wise the erring soul to win!
Go forth into the world's highway!
　　Compel the wanderer to come in!

Toil on, and in thy toil rejoice!
　　For toil comes rest, for exile home;
Soon shalt thou hear the Bridegroom's voice,
　　The midnight peal, "Behold, I come!"

"FAR SOUL FROM HIS STRETCH FEET, SHALT CALL HIS MEN."

Blest are the pure in heart,
  For they shall see their God ;
The secret of the Lord is theirs ;
  Their soul is Christ's abode.

He to the lowly soul
  Doth still himself impart,
And for His dwelling and His throne,
  Chooseth the pure in heart.

Lord! we Thy presence seek ;
  May ours this blessing be ;
Oh, give the pure and lowly heart,—
  A temple meet for Thee.

Thine arm, O Lord, in days of old
  Was strong to heal and save;
It triumphed o'er disease and death,
  O'er darkness and the grave.
To Thee they went, the blind, the dumb,
  The palsied and the lame,
The leper with his tainted life,
  The sick with fevered frame.

And lo! Thy touch brought life and health,
  Gave speech, and strength, and sight;
And youth renewed and frenzy calmed
  Owned Thee, the Lord of light.
And now, O Lord, be near to bless,
  Almighty as of yore,
In crowded street, by restless couch,
  As by Gennesareth's shore.

Though love and might no longer heal
  By touch, or word, or look;
Though they who do Thy work must read
  Thy laws in nature's book;
Yet come to heal the sick man's soul,
  Come, cleanse the leprous taint,
Give joy and peace, where all is strife,
  And strength, where all is faint.

Be Thou our great deliverer still,
  Thou Lord of life and death,
Restore and quicken, soothe and bless
  With Thine almighty breath.
To hands that work and eyes that see,
  Give wisdom's heavenly lore,
That whole and sick, and weak and strong,
  May praise Thee evermore.

"I WILL, BE THOU CLEAN."

Behold, the Master passeth by!
Oh, seest thou not His pleading eye?
With low, sad voice He calleth thee,
"Leave this vain world, and follow Me."

O soul, bowed down with harrowing care,
Hast thou no thought for heaven to spare?
From earthly toils lift up thine eye;
Behold, the Master passeth by!

One heard Him calling long ago,
And straightway left all things below,
Counting his earthly gain as loss
For Jesus and His blessèd cross.

That "follow Me" his faithful ear
Seemed every day afresh to hear:
Its echoes stirred his spirit still,
And fired his hope, and nerved his will.

God gently calls us every day:
Why should we then our bliss delay?
He calls to heaven and endless light:
Why should we love the dreary night?

Praise, Lord, to Thee, for Matthew's call,
At which he rose and left his all:
Thou, Lord, e'en now art calling me;
I will leave all, and follow Thee.

"FOLLOW ME."

Faith is a living power from heaven,
Which grasps the promise God has given;
A trust that cannot be o'erthrown,
Securely fixed on Christ alone.

Faith finds in Christ whate'er we need,
To save and strengthen, guide and feed;
Strong in His grace, it joys to share;
His cross, in hope His crown to wear.

Faith feels the Spirit's kindling breath,
In hope and love that conquer death;
Faith brings us to delight in God,
And blesses e'en His smiting rod.

Such faith in us, O God, implant,
And to our prayers Thy favor grant,
In Jesus Christ, Thy saving Son,
Who is our Fount of health alone.

"VERILY I SAY UNTO YOU, I HAVE NOT FOUND SO GREAT
FAITH, NO, NOT IN ISRAEL."

Fierce was the storm of wind,
  The surging waves ran high,
Failed the disciples hearts with fear,
  Though Thou, their Lord, was nigh.

But at the stern rebuke
  Of Thy almighty word,
The wind was hushed, the billows ceased
  And owned Thee God and Lord.

So, now, when depths of sin
  Our soul with terrors fill,
Arise, and be our helper, Lord,
  And speak Thy "Peace, be still."

When death's dark sea we cross,
  Be with us in Thy power,
Nor let the water-floods prevail
  In that dread final hour.

And, when amid the signs,
  Which speak Thine Advent near,
The roaring of the sea and waves
  Fills faithless hearts with fear.

May we all undismayed
  The raging tempest see,
Lift up our heads and hail with joy
  Thy great Epiphany.

"PEACE, BE STILL."

Faith, like an unsuspecting child,
  Serenely resting on its mother's arm,
Reposing every care upon her God,
  Sleeps on His bosom, and expects no harm.

Receives with joy the promises He makes,
  Nor questions of His purpose or His power;
She does not doubting ask, "Can this be so?"
  The Lord has said it, and there needs no more.

However deep be the mysterious word,
  However dark, she disbelieves it not;
Where Reason would examine, Faith obeys,
  And "It is written" answers every doubt.

In vain with rude and overwhelming force
  Conscience repeats her tale of misery;
And powers infernal, wakeful to destroy
  Urge the worn spirit to despair and die.

As evening's pale and solitary star
  But brightens while the darkness gathers round,
So Faith, unmoved amidst surrounding storms
  Is fairest seen in darkness most profound.

"DAUGHTER, BE OF GOOD COMFORT; THY FAITH
HATH MADE THEE WHOLE."

Behold, where, in a mortal form,
  Appears each grace divine!
The virtues, all in Jesus met,
  With mildest radiance shine.

To spread the rays of heavenly light,
  To give the mourner joy,
To preach glad tidings to the poor,
  Was His divine employ.

AND HER SPIRIT CAME AGAIN.

Saviour! I follow on,
   Guided by Thee,
Seeing not yet the hand
   That leadeth me;
Hushed be my heart and still,
Fear I no further ill,
Only to meet Thy will
   My will shall be.

Riven the rock for me
   Thirst to relieve,
Manna from heaven falls
   Fresh every eve;
Never a want severe
Causeth my eye a tear,
But Thou dost whisper near,
   "Only believe!"

Often to Marah's brink
   Have I been brought;
Shrinking the cup to drink,
   Help I have sought;
And with the prayer's ascent,
Jesus the branch hath rent,
Quickly relief hath sent,
   Sweetening the draught.

Saviour! I long to walk
   Closer with Thee ;
Led by Thy guiding hand,
   Ever to be;
Constantly near Thy side,
Quickened and purified,
Living for Him who died
   Freely for me.

Would you see Jesus? come with prayer,
  And heart repentant, to His feet;
None who will rightly seek Him there,
  Shall fail His face of love to greet.

Would you see Jesus? come with faith,
  And search the word His grace hath given,
For help and guidance in the path
  That leads to His abode in heaven.

Would you see Jesus? day by day
  Let thought and converse be on high,
And hastening on the heavenward way,
  With Jesus live, with Jesus die.

"Go, preach my gospel," saith the Lord;
  "Bid the whole earth my grace receive;
He shall be saved that trusts my word,
  And he condemned who'll not believe.

"I'll make your great commission known;
  And ye shall prove my gospel true,
By all the works that I have done,
  By all the wonders ye shall do.

"Teach all the nations my commands;
  I'm with you till the world shall end;
All power is trusted in my hands;
  I can destroy, and I defend."

Zion, awake! behold the day!
Put on thy beautiful array!
Church of our God, arise and shine,
Bright with the beams of truth divine.

Soon shall thy radiance stream afar,
Wide as the heathen nations are;
Gentiles and kings thy light shall view;
All shall admire, and love thee too.

Lord, speak to me, that I may speak
   In living echoes of Thy tone ;
As Thou hast sought, so let me seek,
   Thy erring children lost and lone.

Oh, lead me, Lord, that I may lead
   The wandering and the wavering feet ;
Oh, feed me, Lord, that I may feed
   Thy hungering ones with manna sweet.

Oh, strengthen me, that while I stand
   Firm on the Rock, and strong in Thee,
I may stretch out a loving hand
   To wrestlers with the troubled sea.

Oh, teach me, Lord, that I may teach
   The precious things Thou dost impart;
And wing my words that they may reach
   The hidden depths of many a heart.

Oh, give Thine own sweet rest to me,
   That I may speak with soothing power
A word in season, as from Thee,
   To weary ones in needful hour.

Oh, fill me with Thy fullness, Lord,
   Until my very heart o'erflow
In kindling thought and glowing word,
   Thy love to tell, Thy praise to show.

Oh, use me, Lord, use even me,
   Just as Thou wilt, and when, and where,
Until Thy blessèd face I see,
   Thy rest, Thy joy, Thy glory share.

Not to the terrors of the Lord,
  The tempest, fire, and smoke:
Not to the thunder of that word
  Which God on Sinai spoke:

But we are come to Sion's hill,
  The city of our God;
Where milder words declare His will,
  And spread His love abroad.

Behold the innumerable host
  Of angels clothed in light:
Behold the spirits of the just,
  Whose faith is changed to sight.

Behold the blest assembly there
  Whose names are writ in heaven;
Hear God, the Judge of all, declare
  Their sins, through Christ, forgiven.

Angels, and living saints, and dead,
  But one communion make:
All join in Christ, their living Head,
  And of His love partake.

THE LAW.

How shall the sons of men appear,
Great God! before Thine awful bar?
How may the guilty hope to find
Acceptance with th' eternal Mind?

Not vows, nor groans, nor broken cries,
Not the most costly sacrifice,
Not infant blood, profusely spilt,
Will expiate a sinner's guilt.

Thy blood, dear Jesus, Thine alone,
Hath sovereign virtue to atone:
Here will we rest our only plea,
When we approach, Great God! to Thee.

"NO MAN COMETH UNTO THE FATHER BUT BY ME."

Just as I am, without one plea,
But that Thy blood was shed for me,
And that Thou bidd'st me come to Thee,
    O Lamb of God, I come.

Just as I am, and waiting not
To rid my soul of one dark blot,
To Thee, whose blood can cleanse each spot,
    O Lamb of God, I come.

Just as I am, though tossed about
With many a conflict, many a doubt,
Fightings and fears within, without,
    O Lamb of God, I come.

Just as I am, poor, wretched, blind ;
Sight, riches, healing of the mind,
Yea, all I need, in Thee to find,
    O Lamb of God, I come.

Just as I am: Thou wilt receive,
Wilt welcome, pardon, cleanse, relieve ;
Because Thy promise I believe,
    O Lamb of God, I come.

Just as I am, Thy love unknown
Has broken every barrier down ;
Now to be Thine, yea, Thine alone,
    O Lamb of God, I come.

It is not death to die ;
  To leave this weary road,
And 'midst the brotherhood on high
  To be at home with God.

It is not death to close
  The eye long dimmed by tears,
And wake, in glorious repose
  To spend eternal years.

It is not death to bear
  The wrench that sets us free
From dungeon chain, to breathe the air
  Of boundless liberty.

It is not death to fling
  Aside this sinful dust,
And rise, on strong, exulting wing,
  To live among the just.

Jesus, Thou Prince of life !
  Thy chosen cannot die ;
Like Thee, they conquer in the strife,
  To reign with Thee on high.

AND SHE SAID—"THE HEAD OF JOHN THE BAPTIST."

Ye wretched, hungry, starving poor,
  Behold a royal feast,
Where Mercy spreads her bounteous store
  For every humble guest.

There Jesus stands with open arms;
  He calls—He bids you come:
Though guilt restrains, and fear alarms,
  Behold there yet is room.

O, come, and with His children taste
  The blessings of His love;
While hope expects the sweet repast
  Of nobler joys above.

There, with united heart and voice,
  Before th' eternal throne,
Ten thousand thousand souls rejoice,
  In songs on earth unknown.

And yet ten thousand thousand more
  Are welcome still to come;
Ye longing souls, the grace adore
  And enter while there's room.

"I AM THE LIVING BREAD WHICH CAME DOWN FROM HEAVEN."

Welcome to me the darkest night,
If there the Saviour's presence bright
Beam forth upon the soul dismayed,
And say, " 'Tis I, be not afraid."

Welcome the fiercest waves that roll
Their deepening floods to whelm my soul,
If He rebuke the storm of ill,
And bid the tempest, " Peace, be still."

Welcome the thorniest path, if there
The print-marks of His feet appear;
If in His footsteps we may tread,
And follow where our Lord hath led.

I will not ask what else is mine,
If Thou, O Lord, account me Thine;
For what but joy can be my lot,
If Thou, my God, reject me not?

Thou, Who in darkness walking didst appear
Upon the waves, and Thy disciples cheer,
Come, Lord, in lonesome days, when storms assail,
And earthly hopes and human succors fail:
When all is dark may we behold Thee nigh,
And hear Thy voice—" Fear not, for it is I."

"BE OF GOOD CHEER: IT IS I: BE NOT AFRAID."

Jesus, lover of my soul,
　　Let me to Thy bosom fly
While the billows near me roll,
　　While the tempest still is high.
Hide me, O my Saviour! hide,
　　Till the storm of life is past ;
Safe into the haven guide ;
　　Oh, receive my soul at last!

Other refuge have I none;
　　Hangs my helpless soul on Thee ;
Leave, ah! leave me not alone,
　　Still support and comfort me.
All my trust on Thee is stayed ;
　　All my help from Thee I bring ;
Cover my defenceless head
　　With the shadow of Thy wing.

Thou, O Christ, art all I want ;
　　More than all in Thee I find ;
Raise the fallen, cheer the faint,
　　Heal the sick, and lead the blind.
Just and holy is Thy name,
　　I am all unrighteousness ;
Vile and full of sin I am,
　　Thou art full of truth and grace.

Plenteous grace with Thee is found,—
　　Grace to pardon all my sin ;
Let the healing streams abound,
　　Make and keep me pure within ;
Thou of life the fountain art,
　　Freely let me take of Thee ;
Spring Thou up within my heart,
　　Rise to all eternity.

"Thou art the Christ, O Lord,
    The Son of God most high!"
Forever be adored
    That name in earth and sky,
In which, though mortal strength may fail,
The saints of God at last prevail!

Oh, surely He was blest
    With blessedness unpriced,
Who, taught of God, confessed
    The Godhead in the Christ;
For of thy church, Lord, Thou didst own
Thy saint a true foundation stone.

"THOU ART PETER, AND UPON THIS ROCK I WILL BUILD MY CHURCH."

Oh, wondrous type! Oh, vision fair
Of glory that the church shall share,
Which Christ upon the mountain shows,
Where brighter than the sun He glows.

From age to age the tale declare
How with the three disciples there,
Where Moses and Elias meet,
The Lord holds converse high and sweet.

The Law and Prophets then have place,
Two chosen witnesses of grace :
The Father's voice, from out the cloud,
Proclaims His only Son aloud.

With shining face and bright array,
Christ deigns to manifest to-day
What glory shall be thine above,
Who joy in God with perfect love.

And faithful hearts are raised on high
By this great vision's mystery :
For which in joyful strains we raise
The voice of prayer, the hymn of praise.

O Father with the eternal Son,
And Holy Spirit, ever one,
Vouchsafe to bring us by Thy grace
To see Thy glory face to face.

What is the world ? a wildering maze
Where sin hath tracked ten thousand ways
    Her victims to ensnare ;
All broad, and winding, and aslope,
All tempting with perfidious hope
    All ending in despair.

Millions of pilgrims throng these roads,
Bearing their baubles or their loads
    Down to eternal night ;
The only path that never bends,
Narrow, and rough, and steep ascends
    From darkness into light.

Is there no guide to show that path ?
The Bible!—He alone who hath
    The Bible, need not stray ;
But he who hath and will not give
That light of life to all that live,
    Himself shall lose the way.

THE PRODIGAL'S DEPARTURE.

Return, O wanderer, now return,
  And seek thy Father's face!
Those new desires, which in thee burn,
  Were kindled by His grace.

Return, O wanderer, now return!
  He hears thy humble sigh;
He sees thy softened spirit mourn,
  When no one else is nigh.

Return, O wanderer, now return!
  Thy Saviour bids thee live;
Go to His bleeding feet, and learn
  How freely he'll forgive.

Return, O wanderer, now return,
  And wipe the falling tear!
Thy Father calls—no longer mourn:
  His love invites thee near.

WHEN HE CAME TO HIMSELF.

Love divine, all love excelling, —
  Joy of heaven, to earth come down!
Fix in us Thy humble dwelling,
  All Thy faithful mercies crown:
Jesus! Thou art all compassion,
  Pure unbounded love Thou art;
Visit us with Thy salvation,
  Enter every trembling heart.

Breathe, oh, breathe Thy loving Spirit
  Into every troubled breast!
Let us all in Thee inherit,
  Let us find Thy promised rest:
Come, almighty to deliver,
  Let us all Thy life receive!
Speedily return, and never,
  Never more Thy temples leave!

Finish then Thy new creation,
  Pure, unspotted may we be:
Let us see our whole salvation
  Perfectly secured by Thee!
Changed from glory into glory,
  Till in heaven we take our place;
Till we cast our crowns before Thee,
  Lost in wonder, love, and praise.

BUT WHEN HE WAS YET A GREAT WAY OFF HIS FATHER SAW HIM, AND HAD COMPASSION, AND RAN AND FELL ON HIS NECK AND KISSED HIM.

Is this the kind return,
    Are these the thanks we owe,
Thus to abuse eternal love,
    Whence all our blessings flow ?

To what a stubborn frame,
    Has sin reduced our mind!
What strange rebellious wretches we,
    And God as strangely kind!

Turn, turn us, mighty God,
    And mould our souls afresh;
Break, sovereign grace, these hearts of stone,
    And give us hearts of flesh.

"WERE THERE NOT TEN CLEANSED? BUT WHERE ARE THE NINE?"

Fountain of grace, rich, full, and free,
What need I that is not in Thee ?
Full pardon, strength to meet the day,
And peace which none can take away.

Doth sickness fill the heart with fear ?
'Tis sweet to know that Thou art near,
Am I with dread of justice tried ?
'Tis sweet to feel that Christ hath died.

In life, Thy promises of aid
Forbid my heart to be afraid;
In death, peace gently veils the eyes;
Christ rose, and I shall surely rise.

O all-sufficient Saviour, be
This all-sufficiency to me ;
Nor pain, nor sin, nor death can harm
The weakest shielded by Thine arm.

"WHOSOEVER DRINKETH OF THE WATER THAT I SHALL GIVE HIM SHALL
NEVER THIRST."

Call them in! the poor, the wretched,
  Sin-stained wanderers from the fold;
Peace and pardon freely offer!
  Can you weigh their worth with gold?
Call them in! the weak, the weary,
  Laden with the doom of sin;
Bid them come and rest in Jesus!
  He is waiting: call them in!

Call them in! the Jew, the Gentile;
  Bid the stranger to the feast!
Call them in, the rich, the noble,
  From the highest to the least.
Call them in! the broken-hearted,
  Cowering 'neath the brand of shame;
Speak love's message low and tender!
  'Twas for sinners Jesus came.

"HE THAT IS WITHOUT SIN AMONG YOU," LET HIM FIRST CAST A STONE AT HER."

O Love Divine! that stooped to share
  Our sharpest pang, our bitterest tear,
On Thee we cast each earth-born care,
  We smile at pain when Thou art near.

Though long the weary way we tread,
  And sorrow crown each lingering year,
No path we shun, no darkness dread,
  Our hearts still whispering, Thou art near.

When drooping pleasure turns to grief,
  And trembling faith is changed to fear,
The murmuring wind, the quivering leaf,
  Shall softly tell us Thou art near.

On Thee we fling our burdening woe,
  O Love Divine, forever dear;
Content to suffer while we know,
  Living or dying, Thou art near.

"WHERE ARE THOSE THINE ACCUSERS? HATH NO MAN
    CONDEMNED THEE?"

"NO MAN LORD."

" NEITHER DO I CONDEMN THEE ; GO, AND SIN NO MORE.'

O Light, whose beams illumine all
  From twilight dawn to perfect day,
Shine Thou before the shadows fall,
  That lead our wandering feet astray:
At morn and eve Thy radiance pour,
That youth may love, and age adore.

O Way, through Whom our souls draw near
  To you eternal home of peace,
Where perfect love shall cast out fear,
  And earth's vain toil and wandering cease:
In strength or weakness may we see
Our heavenward path, O Lord, through Thee

O Truth, before whose shrine we bow,
  Thou priceless pearl for all who seek,
To Thee our earliest strength we vow ;
  Thy love will bless the pure and meek :
When dreams or mists beguile our sight,
Turn Thou our darkness into light.

O Life, the well that ever flows
  To slake the thirst of those that faint,
Thy power to bless, what seraph knows ?
  Thy joy supreme, what words can paint ?
In earth's last hour of fleeting breath
Be Thou our conquerer over death.

O Light, O Way, O Truth, O Life,
  O Jesus, born mankind to save,
Give Thou Thy peace in deadliest strife ;
  Shed Thou Thy calm on stormiest wave :
Be Thou our hope, our joy, our dread,
Lord of the living and the dead.

"I AM THE LIGHT, I AM THE WAY, THE TRUTH AND THE LIFE."

There's a friend for little children
  Above the bright blue sky,
A friend Who never changes,
  Whose love will never die ;
Our earthly friends may fail us,
  And change with changing years.
This friend is always worthy
  Of that dear Name He bears.

There's a rest for little children,
  Above the bright blue sky,
Who love the blessèd Saviour,
  And to the Father cry ;
A rest from every turmoil,
  From sin and sorrow free,
Where every little pilgrim
  Shall rest eternally.

There's a home for little children
  Above the bright blue sky,
Where Jesus reigns in glory,
  A home of peace and joy ;
No home on earth is like it,
  Nor can with it compare;
For every one is happy,
  Nor could be happier there.

"SUFFER THE LITTLE CHILDREN TO COME UNTO ME,
AND FORBID THEM NOT:"

There's a song for little children
  Above the bright blue sky,
A song that will not weary,
  Though sung continually ;
A song which even angels
  Can never, never sing :
They know not Christ as Saviour,
  But worship him as King.

There's a crown for little children
  Above the bright blue sky,
And all who look for Jesus
  Shall wear it bye and bye,
All, all above is treasured
  And found in Christ alone:
Lord, grant Thy little children
  To know Thee as their own.

"FOR OF SUCH IS THE KINGDOM OF GOD."

When Jesus left His Father's throne,
  He chose an humble birth;
Like us, unhonored and unknown,
  He came to dwell on earth.
Like Him may we be found below,
  In wisdom's path of peace ;
Like Him in grace and knowledge grow,
  As years and strength increase.

Sweet were His words and kind His look,
  When mothers round Him pressed ;
Their infants in His arms He took,
  And on His bosom blessed.
Safe from the world's alluring harms,
  Beneath His watchful eye,
Thus in the circle of His arms
  May we forever lie.

When Jesus into Salem rode,
  The children sang around ;
For joy they plucked the palms, and strowed
  Their garments on the ground.
Hosanna our glad voices raise,
  Hosanna to our King!
Should we forget our Saviour's praise,
  The stones themselves would sing.

Saviour, like a shepherd lead us,
  Much we need Thy tender care ;
In Thy pleasant pastures feed us ;
  For our use Thy folds prepare :
    Blessèd Jesus!
Thou hast bought us, Thine we are.

Thou hast promised to receive us,
  Poor and sinful though we be ;
Thou hast mercy to relieve us,
  Grace to cleanse, and power to free :
    Blessèd Jesus!
Let us early turn to Thee.

Early let us seek Thy favor,
  Early let us learn Thy will ;
Do Thou, Lord, our only Saviour,
  With Thy love our bosoms fill :
    Blessèd Jesus!
Thou hast loved us : love us still.

And must I part with all I have,
My dearest Lord, for Thee!
It is but right! since thou has done
Much more than this for me.

Ten thousand worlds, ten thousand lives,
How worthless they appear,
Compared with Thee, supremely good!
Divinely bright and fair.

Thy favor, Lord, is endless life, -
Let me that life obtain,
Then I renounce all earthly joys,
And glory in my gain.

"HOW HARDLY SHALL THEY THAT HAVE RICHES ENTER INTO THE KINGDOM OF GOD."

Lord, forever at Thy side
  Let my place and portion be ;
Strip me of the robe of pride,
  Clothe me with humility.

Meekly may my soul receive,
  All Thy Spirit hath revealed ;
Thou hast spoken; I believe,
  Though the oracle be sealed.

Humble as a little child,
  Weanèd from the mother's breast,
By no subleties beguiled,
  On Thy faithful word I rest.

Israel now and evermore,
  In the Lord Jehovah trust ;
Him, in all His ways adore,
  Wise, and wonderful, and just.

Jesus, engrave it on my heart,
That Thou the one thing needful art;
I could from all things parted be,
But never, never, Lord, from Thee.

Needful is Thy most precious blood,
To reconcile my soul to God;
Needful is Thy indulgent care;
Needful Thy all-prevailing prayer.

Needful Thy presence, dearest Lord,
True peace and comfort to afford;
Needful Thy promise, to impart
Fresh life and vigor to my heart.

Needful art Thou, my guide, my stay,
Through all life's dark and weary way;
Nor less in death Thou'lt needful be,
To bring my spirit home to Thee.

Then needful still, my God, my King,
Thy name eternally I'll sing!
Glory and praise be ever His,
The one thing needful Jesus is!

"BUT ONE THING IS NEEDFUL."

Did Christ o'er sinners weep,
   And shall our cheeks be dry ?
Let floods of penitential grief
   Burst forth from every eye.

The Son of God in tears,
   Angels with wonder see!
Be thou astonished, O my soul,
   He shed those tears for thee.

He wept that we might weep,
   Each sin demands a tear;
In heaven alone no sin is found,
   And there's no weeping there.

"O JERUSALEM! JERUSALEM!—"

When Lazarus left his charnel-cave,
   And home to Mary's house return'd,
   Was this demanded, –if he yearn'd
To hear her weeping by his grave?

"Where wert thou, brother, those four days?"
   There lives no record of reply,
   Which telling what it is to die
Had surely added praise to praise.

" LAZARUS, COME FORTH."

From every house the neighbors met,
  The streets were fill'd with joyful sound,
  A solemn gladness even crown'd
The purple brows of Olivet.

Behold a man raised up by Christ!
  The rest remaineth unreveal'd;
  He told it not; or something seal'd
The lips of that Evangelist.

Her eyes are homes of silent prayer,
  Nor other thought her mind admits,
  But, he was dead, and there he sits,
And he that brought him back is there.

Then one deep love doth supersede
  All other, when her ardent gaze
  Roves from the living brother's face,
And rests upon the Life indeed.

All subtle thought, all curious fears,
  Borne down by gladness so complete,
  She bows, she bathes the Saviour's feet
With costly spikenard and with tears.

Thrice blest whose lives are faithful prayers,
  Whose loves in higher love endure ;
  What souls possess themselves so pure,
Or is there blessedness like theirs ?

We are on our journey home,
  Where Christ our Lord is gone ;
We shall meet around His throne,
  When he makes His people one,
    In the new Jerusalem.

We can see that distant home,
  Though clouds rise dark between :
Faith views the radiant dome,
  And a lustre flashes keen
    From the new Jerusalem.

Oh, holy, heavenly home!
  Oh, rest eternal there!
When shall the exiles come,
  Where they cease from earthly care,
    In the new Jerusalem.

Our hearts are breaking now
  Those mansions fair to see ;
O Lord! Thy heavens bow,
  And raise us up with Thee,
    To the new Jerusalem.

Scorn not the slightest word or deed,
  Nor deem it void of power ;
There's fruit in each wind-wafted seed,
  That waits its natal hour.

A whispered word may touch the heart,
  And call it back to life ;
A look of love bid sin depart,
  And still unholy strife.

No act falls fruitless; none can tell
  How vast its power may be,
Nor what results infolded dwell
  Within it silently.

Work on, despair not, bring thy mite,
  Nor care how small it be ;
God is with all that serve the right,
  The holy, true, and free.

"OF A TRUTH, THIS POOR WIDOW HATH CAST IN MORE THAN THEY ALL."

"Late, late, so late! and dark the night and chill!
Late, late, so late! but we can enter still,
    Too late, too late! ye cannot enter now.

"No light had we: for that we do repent;
And learning this, the bridegroom will repent.
    Too late, too late! ye cannot enter now.

"No light: so late! and dark and chill the night!
O let us in that we may find the light!
Too late, too late! ye cannot enter now.

"Have we not heard the bridegroom is so sweet?
O let us in, tho' late, to kiss his feet!
No, no, too late! ye cannot enter now."

AFTERWARD CAME ALSO THE OTHER VIRGINS, SAYING
"LORD, LORD, OPEN UNTO US."

More love to Thee, O Christ!
  More love to Thee!
Hear Thou the prayer I make
  On bended knee:
This is my earnest plea,
More love, O Christ to Thee!
  More love to Thee!

Once earthly joy I craved,
  Sought peace and rest;
Now Thee alone I seek;
  Give what is best:
This all my prayer shall be,
More love, O Christ, to Thee,
  More love to Thee!

Let sorrow do its work,
  Send grief and pain;
Sweet are Thy messengers,
  Sweet their refrain,
When they can sing with me,
More love, O Christ, to Thee,
  More love to Thee.

Then shall my latest breath
  Whisper Thy praise;
This be the parting cry
  My heart shall raise,
This still its prayer shall be,
More love, O Christ, to Thee,
  More love to Thee.

"TO WHOM LITTLE IS FORGIVEN, THE SAME LOVETH LITTLE."

'Twas on that dark, that doleful night,
    When powers of earth and hell arose
Against the Son of God's delight,
    And friends betrayed Him to His foes.

Before the mournful scene began,
    He took the bread, and blessed, and brake:
What love through all His actions ran!
    What wondrous words of grace He spake!

"This is my body, broke for sin ;
    Receive and eat the living food:"
Then took the cup, and blessed the wine ;
    "'Tis the new covenant in my blood."

"Do this," he cried, "till time shall end,
    In memory of your dying Friend;
Meet at my table, and record
    The love of your departed Lord."

Jesus, Thy feast we celebrate ;
    We show Thy death, we sing Thy name,
Till Thou return, and we shall eat
    The marriage supper of the Lamb.

The Saviour! oh, what endless charms
    Dwell in the blissful sound!
Its influence every fear disarms,
    And spreads sweet comfort round.

The almighty Former of the skies
    Stooped to our vile abode ;
While angel viewed with wondering eyes
    And hailed the incarnate God.

Oh! the rich depths of love divine!
    Of bliss a boundless store!
Dear Saviour, let me call Thee mine ;
    I cannot wish for more.

On Thee alone my hope relies
    Beneath Thy cross I fall;
My Lord, my Life, my Sacrifice,
    My Saviour, and my All.

"IF I THEN, YOUR LORD AND MASTER HAVE WASHED YOUR FEET, YE OUGHT ALSO TO WASH ONE ANOTHER'S FEET."

Sure the blest Comforter is nigh,
　'Tis He sustains my fainting heart ;
Else would my hopes forever die,
　And every cheering ray depart.

Whene'er, to call the Saviour mine
　With ardent wish my heart aspires,--
Can it be less than power divine,
That animates these strong desires ?

And, when my cheerful hope can say,—
　I love my God and taste His grace,—
Lord! is it not Thy blissful ray,
　That brings this dawn of sacred peace

Let Thy good Spirit in my heart
　Forever dwell, O God of love!
And light and heavenly peace impart,—
　Sweet earnest of the joys above.

What grace, O Lord, and beauty shone
  Around Thy steps below ;
What patient love was seen in all
  Thy life and death of woe.

For, ever on Thy burdened heart
  A weight of sorrow hung ;
Yet no ungentle, murmuring word
  Escaped Thy silent tongue.

Thy foes might hate, despise, revile,
  Thy friends unfaithful prove;
Unwearied in forgiveness still,
  Thy heart could only love.

Oh, give us hearts to love like Thee!
  Like Thee, O Lord, to grieve
Far more for others' sins than all
  The wrongs that we receive.

One with Thyself, may every eye,
  In us, Thy brethren, see
The gentleness and grace that spring
  From union, Lord! with Thee.

"NEITHER PRAY I FOR THESE ALONE, BUT FOR THEM ALSO WHICH SHALL BELIEVE ON ME THROUGH THEIR WORD."

He knelt: the Saviour knelt and prayed,
  When but His Father's eye
Looked thro' the lonely garden's shade,
  On that dread agony ;
The Lord of all above, beneath,
Was bowed with sorrow unto death.

The sun set in a fearful hour,
  The skies might well grow dim,
When this mortality had power
  So to o'ershadow Him!
That He who gave man's breath might know
The very depths of human woe.

He knew them all, the doubt, the strife,
  The faint, perplexing dread,
The mists that hang o'er parting life,
  All darkened round His head ;
And the Deliverer knelt to pray :—
  Yet passed it not, that cup, away.

It passed not, though the stormy wave
  Had sunk beneath His tread ;
It passed not, tho' to Him the grave
  Had yielded up its dead:
But there was sent Him from on high
A gift of strength for man to die.

And was His mortal hour beset
  With anguish and dismay ?
How may we meet our conflict yet
  In the dark, narrow way ?
How but thro' Him, that path Who trod ?
Save or we perish, Son of God!

Go to dark Gethsemane,
  Ye that feel the tempter's power ;
Your Redeemer's conflict see,
  Watch with Him one bitter hour ;
Turn not from His griefs away,
Learn of Jesus Christ to pray.

Follow to the judgment-hall;
  View the Lord of life arraigned ;
Oh, the wormwood and the gall!
  Oh, the pangs His soul sustained!
Shun not suffering, shame, or loss;
Learn of Him to bear the cross.

Calvary's mournful mountain climb ;
  There, adoring at His feet,
Mark that miracle of time,
  God's own sacrifice complete:
"It is finished," hear Him cry;—
Learn of Jesus Christ to die.

Early hasten to the tomb,
  Where they laid His breathless clay;
All is solitude and gloom
  Who hath taken Him away ?
Christ is risen;—He meets our eyes;
Saviour, teach us so to rise!

O suffering Friend of human-kind!
  How, as the fatal hour drew near,
Came thronging on Thy holy mind
  The images of grief and fear!

Gethsemane's sad midnight scene,
  The faithless friends, the exulting foes,
The thorny crown, the insult keen,
  The scourge, the cross, before Thee rose.

Onward, like Thee, thro' scorn and dread,
  May we our Father's call obey,
Steadfast the path of duty tread,
  And rise, through death, to endless day.

Oh, who like Thee, so calm, so bright,
Lord Jesus Christ, Thou Light of Light!
Oh, who like Thee, did ever go
So patient through a world of woe!
So meek, so lowly, yet so high,
So glorious in humility.

O wondrous Lord, our souls would be
Still more and more conformed to Thee;
Would lose the pride, the taint of sin,
That burns these fevered veins within:
And learn of Thee, the lowly One,
And like Thee all our journey run.

Oh, grant us ever on the road
To trace the footsteps of our God:
That when Thou shalt appear, arrayed
In light to judge the quick and dead,
We may to life immortal soar,
Through Thee, Who livest evermore.

"JUDAS BETRAYEST THOU THE SON OF MAN WITH A KISS?"

Not to condemn the sons of men,
   Did Christ, the Son of God, appear;
No weapons in His hands are seen,
   No flaming sword, nor thunder there.

Such was the pity of our God,
   He loved the race of men so well,
He sent His Son to bear our load
   Of sins, and save our souls from hell.

Sinners, believe the Saviour's word ;
   Trust in His mighty name, and live:
A thousand joys His lips afford,
   His hands a thousand blessings give.

"PUT UP THY SWORD: THE CUP WHICH MY FATHER HATH
GIVEN ME, SHALL I NOT DRINK IT?"

Shall the vile race of flesh and blood
Contend with their Creator, God?
Shall mortal worms presume to be
More holy, wise, or just, than He?

Behold! he puts His trust in none
Of all the spirits round His throne;
Their natures, when compared with His,
Are neither holy, just, nor wise.

But how much meaner things are they
Who spring from dust, and dwell in clay;
Touched by the finger of Thy wrath,
We faint and vanish like the moth.

From night to day, from day to night,
We die by thousands in Thy sight;
Buried in dust whole nations lie,
Like a forgotten vanity.

Almighty Power, to Thee we bow;
How frail are we! how glorious Thou!
No more the sons of earth shall dare
With an eternal God compare.

AND STRAIGHTWAY IN THE MORNING, THE CHIEF PRIESTS HELD A CONSULTATION
WITH THE ELDERS AND SCRIBES—BOUND JESUS, CARRIED HIM
AWAY AND DELIVERED HIM TO PILATE.

Behold the Man! How glorious He!
  Before His foes He stands unawed,
And without wrong or blasphemy,
  He claims equality with God.

Behold the Man! by all condemned,
  Assaulted by a host of foes,
His person and His claims contemned,
  A man of sufferings and of woes.

Behold the Man! He stands alone ;
  His foes are ready to devour;
Not one of all His friends will own
  Their Master in this trying hour.

Behold the Man! So weak He seems,
  His awful words inspire no fear ;
But soon must he who now blasphemes
  Before His judgment seat appear.

Behold the Man! Though scorned below,
  He bears the greatest name above ;
The angels at His footstool bow,
  And all His royal claims approve.

Thrice fallen, thrice restored!
   The bitter lesson learnt,
That heart for Thee, O Lord,
   With triple ardor burnt.
The cross He took He laid not down
Until He grasped the martyr's crown.

Oh bright, triumphant faith!
   Oh courage void of fears!
Oh love, most strong in death!
   Oh penitential tears!
By these, Lord, keep us lest we fall,
And make us go where Thou shalt call.

AND PETER REMEMBERED THE WORD OF JESUS; AND WHEN
HE THOUGHT THEREON, HE WEPT.

Oh! where shall rest be found—
  Rest for the weary soul?
'Twere vain the ocean's depths to sound,
  Or pierce to either pole.

The world can never give
  The bliss for which we sigh:
'Tis not the whole of life to live,
  Nor all of death to die.

Beyond this vale of tears
  There is a life above,
Unmeasured by the flight of years;
  And all that life is love.

There is a death whose pang
  Outlasts the fleeting breath:
Oh, what eternal horrors hang
  Around the second death.

Lord God of truth and grace!
  Teach us that death to shun:
Lest we be banished from Thy face,
  And evermore undone.

"I HAVE BETRAYED THE INNOCENT BLOOD!"
"WHAT IS THAT TO US? SEE THOU TO THAT."

Jesus, whom angel hosts adore,
  Became a man of griefs for me ;
In love, though rich, becoming poor,
  That I through him enriched might be.

Though Lord of all, above, below,
  He went to Olivet for me:
There drank my cup of wrath and woe,
  When bleeding in Gethsemane.

The ever-blessèd Son of God
  Went up to Calvary for me ;
There paid my debt, there bore my load,
  In His own body on the tree.

Jesus, whose dwelling is the skies,
  Went down into the grave for me ;
There overcame my enemies,
  There won the glorious victory.

'Tis finished all: the vail is rent,
  The welcome sure, the access free;—
Now then, we leave our banishment,
  O Father, to return to Thee!

I see the crowd in Pilate's hall,
  I mark their wrathful mien ;
Their shouts of "crucify" appall,
  With blasphemy between.

And of that shouting multitude
  I feel that I am one;
And in that din of voices rude
  I recognize my own.

I see the scourges tear His back,
  I see the piercing crown,
And of that crowd who smite and mock,
  I feel that I am one.

'Twas I that shed the sacred blood;
  I nailed Him to the tree;
I crucified the Christ of God,
  I joined the mockery.

Yet not the less that blood avails
  To cleanse away my sin :
And not the less that cross prevails
  To give me peace within.

"HAIL, KING OF THE JEWS!"
AND THEY SMOTE HIM WITH THEIR HANDS.

Must Jesus bear the cross alone,
    And all the world go free ?
No, there's a cross for every one,
    And there's a cross for me.

The consecrated cross I'll bear,
    Till death shall set me free,
And then go home my crown to wear,
    For there's a crown for me.

Upon the crystal pavement, down
    At Jesus' piercèd feet,
Joyful, I'll cast my golden crown,
    And His dear name repeat.

And palms shall wave, and harps shall ring,
    Beneath heaven's arches high ;
The Lord that lives, the ransomed sing,
    That lives no more to die.

Oh, precious cross ! oh, glorious crown !
    Oh, resurrection day !
Ye angels, from the stars come down,
    And bear my soul away.

Ev'n though it be a cross
   That raiseth me!
Still all my song shall be,
Nearer, my God, to Thee,
   Nearer to Thee!

Though like the wanderer,
   The sun gone down,
Darkness be over me,
   My rest a stone,
Yet in my dreams I'd be
Nearer, my God, to Thee,
   Nearer to Thee!

There let the way appear
   Steps unto heaven;
All that Thou sendest me,
   In mercy given;
Angels to beckon me
Nearer, my God, to Thee,
   Nearer to Thee!

Then, with my waking thoughts
   Bright with Thy praise,
Out of my stony griefs
   Bethel I'll raise;
So by my woes to be
Nearer, my God, to Thee,
   Nearer to Thee!

Or if, on joyful wing
   Cleaving the sky,
Sun, moon and stars forgot
   Upward I fly,
Still all my song shall be
Nearer, my God, to Thee,
   Nearer to Thee!

"DAUGHTERS OF JERUSALEM, WEEP NOT FOR ME."

'Twas the day when God's Anointed
Died for us the death appointed,
  Bleeding on the dreadful cross ;
Day of darkness, day of terror,
Deadly fruit of ancient error,
  Nature's fall, and Eden's loss !

Haste, prepare the bitter chalice !
Gentile hate and Jewish malice
  Lift the royal Victim high ;
Like the serpent, wonder-gifted,
Which the prophet once uplifted,
  For a sinful world to die.

Conscious of the deed unholy,
Nature's pulses beat more slowly,
  And the sun his light denied ;
Darkness wrapped the sacred city,
And the earth with fear and pity
  Trembled, when the Just One died.

It is finished, Man of sorrows !
From Thy cross our nature borrows
  Strength to bear and conquer thus :
While exalted there we view Thee,
Mighty Sufferer, draw us to Thee,
  Sufferer victorious !

Lord Jesus! when we stand afar,
  And gaze upon Thy holy cross,
In love of Thee, and scorn of self,
  Oh, may we count the world as loss!

When we behold Thy bleeding wounds,
  And the rough way that Thou hast trod,
Make us to hate the load of sin
  That lay so heavy on our God.

O holy Lord, uplifted high,
  With outstretched arms, in mortal woe
Embracing in Thy wondrous love
  The sinful world that lies below ;

Give us an ever-living faith
  To gaze beyond the things we see;
And in the mystery of Thy death
  Draw us and all men unto Thee.

HE DIES!—THE FRIEND OF SINNERS DIES;
LO! SALEM'S DAUGHTERS WEEP AROUND;

When I survey the wondrous cross,
  On which the Prince of glory died,
My richest gain I count but loss,
  And pour contempt on all my pride.

Forbid it, Lord! that I should boast,
  Save in the death of Christ, my God ;
All the vain things that charm me most,
  I sacrifice them to His blood.

See, from His head, His hands, His feet,
  Sorrow and love flow mingled down ;
Did e'er such love and sorrow meet,
  Or thorns compose so rich a crown ?

His dying crimson, like a robe,
  Spreads o'er His body on the tree ;
Then I am dead to all the globe,
  And all the globe is dead to me.

Were the whole realm of nature mine,
  That were a present far too small ;
Love so amazing, so divine,
  Demands my soul, my life, my all.

Rock of Ages, cleft for me!
Let me hide myself in Thee ;
Let the water and the blood,
From Thy wounded side that flowed,
Be of sin the double cure ;
Cleanse me from its guilt and power.

Not the labor of my hands
Can fulfill the laws demands ;
Could my zeal no respite know,
Could my tears forever flow,
All for sin could not atone,
Thou must save, and Thou alone.

Nothing in my hand I bring,
Simply to Thy cross I cling ;
Naked, come to Thee for dress,
Helpless, look to Thee for grace ;
Vile, I to the fountain fly,
Wash me, Saviour, or I die!

While I draw this fleeting breath,
When my eyelids close in death,
When I soar to worlds unknown,
See Thee on Thy judgment-throne,
Rock of Ages, cleft for me!
Let me hide myself in Thee.

Jesus lives!— henceforth is death
   But the gate of life immortal;
This shall calm our trembling breath,
   When we pass its gloomy portal.

Jesus lives!—for us He died ;
   Then, alone to Jesus living,
Pure in heart may we abide,
   Glory to our Saviour giving.

Jesus lives!—our hearts know well,
   Naught from us His love shall sever;
Life, nor death, nor powers of hell,
   Tear us from His keeping ever.

Jesus lives!—to Him the throne
   Over all the world is given:
May we go where He is gone,
   Rest and reign with Him in heaven.

Christ, the Lord, is risen to-day;
Sons of men and angels say:
Raise your joys and triumphs high ;
Sing, ye heavens, and, earth, reply.

Love's redeeming work is done,
Fought the fight, the battle won:
Lo! our Sun's eclipse is o'er ;
Lo! He sets in blood no more.

Vain the stone, the watch, the seal,
Christ hath burst the gates of hell:
Death in vain forbids His rise.
Christ hath opened paradise.

Soar we now where Christ hath led,
Following our exalted Head :
Made like Him, like Him we rise ;
Ours the cross, the grave, the skies.

Mary to the Saviour's tomb
  Hasted at the early dawn ;
Spice she brought and sweet perfume,
  But the Lord she loved had gone.

For awhile she lingering stood,
  Filled with sorrow and surprise,
Trembling, while a crystal flood
  Issued from her weeping eyes.

But her sorrows quickly fled
  When she heard His welcome voice,
Christ had risen from the dead ;
  Now He bids her heart rejoice.

What a change His word can make,
  Turning darkness into day !
Ye who weep for Jesus' sake,
  He will wipe your tears away.

Speak to me, Lord, thyself reveal,
  While here on earth I rove;
Speak to my heart, and let me feel
  The kindling of Thy love.

With Thee conversing, I forget
  All time and toil and care;
Labor is rest, and pain is sweet,
  If Thou, my God, art there.

Thou callest me to seek Thy face ;
  Thy face, O God, I seek,—
Attend the whispers of Thy grace,
  And hear Thee inly speak.

Let this my every hour employ,
  Till I Thy glory see,
Enter into my Master's joy,
  And find my heaven in Thee.

Art thou weary, art thou languid,
　Art thou sore distrest?
"Come to Me," saith One, "and coming,
　　Be at rest."

Hath He marks to lead me to Him,
　If He be my guide?
"In His feet and hands are wound-prints,
　And His side."

If I find Him, if I follow,
　What His guerdon here?
"Many a sorrow, many a labor,
　　Many a tear."

If I still hold closely to Him,
　What hath He at last?
"Sorrow vanquished, labor ended,
　　Jordan past."

If I ask Him to receive me,
　Will He say me nay?
"Not till earth, and not till heaven
　　Pass away."

Finding, following, keeping, struggling,
　Is He sure to bless?
Saints, apostles, prophets, martyrs,
　Answer, "Yes."

Lord, I believe ; Thy power I own ;
  Thy word I would obey;
I wander comfortless and lone,
  When from Thy truth I stray.

Lord, I believe; but gloomy fears
  Sometimes bedim my sight ;
I look to Thee with prayers and tears,
  And cry for strength and light.

Lord, I believe ; but oft, I know
  My faith is cold and weak :
My weakness strengthen, and bestow
  The confidence I seek.

Yes! I believe ; and only Thou
  Canst give my soul relief:
Lord, to Thy truth my spirit bow ;
  " Help Thou mine unbelief!"

"BLESSED ARE THEY THAT HAVE NOT SEEN
AND YET HAVE BELEIVED."

Thou knowest my feebleness,
  Jesus, be Thou my power,—
My help and refuge in distress,
  My fortress and my tower.

Give me to trust in Thee;
  Be Thou my sure abode :
My horn, and rock, and buckler be,
  My Saviour, and my God.

Myself I cannot save,
  Myself I cannot keep;
But strength in Thee I surely have,
  Whose eyelids never sleep.

My soul to Thee alone,
  Now, therefore, I commend :
Lord Jesus, love me as Thine own
  And love me to the end.

"LORD, THOU KNOWEST ALL THINGS; THOU KNOWEST
THAT I LOVE THEE."

"JESUS SAITH UNTO HIM, FEED MY SHEEP."

Our Lord is risen from the dead,
  Our Jesus is gone up on high;
The powers of hell are captive led,
  Dragged to the portals of the sky.
There His triumphal chariot waits,
  And angels chant the solemn lay:—
"Lift up your heads, ye heavenly gates!
  Ye everlasting doors! give way."

Loose all your bars of massy light,
  And wide unfold the ethereal scene:
He claims those mansions as His right;
  Receive the King of glory in.
Who is the King of glory—who?
  The Lord who all our foes o'ercame;
Who sin, and death, and hell o'erthrew;
  And Jesus is the conquerer's name.

Lo! His triumphal chariot waits,
  And angels chant the heavenly lay:—
"Lift up your heads, ye heavenly gates!
  Ye everlasting doors! give way."
Who is the King of glory—who?
  The Lord of boundless power possessed;
The King of saints and angels, too,
  God over all, forever blessed.

AND IT CAME TO PASS, WHILE HE BLESSED THEM, HE WAS PARTED
FROM THEM AND CARRIED UP INTO HEAVEN.

In the cross of Christ I glory,
 Towering o'er the wrecks of time ;
All the light of sacred story
 Gathers round its head sublime.

When the woes of life o'ertake me,
 Hopes deceive, and fears annoy,
Never shall the cross forsake me :
 Lo ! it glows with peace and joy.

When the sun of bliss is beaming
 Light and love upon my way,
From the cross the radiance streaming,
 Adds new lustre to the day.

Bane and blessing, pain and pleasure,
 By the cross are sanctified ;
Peace is there that knows no measure,
 Joys that through all time abide.

In the cross of Christ I glory,
 Towering o'er the wrecks of time ;
All the light of sacred story
 Gathers round its head sublime.

There is a land immortal,
  The beautiful of lands;
Beside its ancient portal
  A silent sentry stands;
He only can undo it,
  And open wide the door;
And mortals who pass through it,
  Are mortals nevermore.

Though dark and drear the passage
  That leadeth to the gate,
Yet grace comes with the message,
  To souls that watch and wait;
And at the time appointed
  A messenger comes down,
And leads the Lord s anointed
  From cross to glory's crown.

Their sighs are lost in singing,
  They're blessèd in their tears;
Their journey heavenward winging,
  They leave on earth their fears:
Death like an angel seemeth;
  "We welcome thee," they cry;
Their face with glory beameth—
  'Tis life for them to die!

My faith looks up to Thee,
Thou Lamb of Calvary,
   Saviour divine!
Now hear me while I pray,
Take all my guilt away,
Oh, let me from this day
   Be wholly Thine!

May Thy rich grace impart
Strength to my fainting heart;
   My zeal inspire;
As Thou hast died for me,
Oh, may my love to Thee
Pure, warm, and changeless be,
   A living fire.

While life's dark maze I tread,
And griefs around me spread,
   Be Thou my guide;
Bid darkness turn to day,
Wipe sorrow's tears away,
Nor let me ever stray
   From Thee aside.

When ends life's transient dream,
When death's cold, sullen stream
   Shall o'er me roll;
Blest Saviour! then, in love,
Fear and distress remove;
Oh, bear me safe above,
   A ransomed soul!